#62
Lake View Terrace Branch
12002 Osborne Street
Lake View Terrace, CA 91342

EXTREME CAREERS™

REFUGEE WORKERS

Janey Levy

rosen publishing's
rosen central®

New York

To the amazing people who work under difficult conditions
to help the world's refugees

Published in 2007 by The Rosen Publishing Group, Inc.
29 East 21st Street, New York, NY 10010

First Edition

Library of Congress Cataloging-in-Publication Data

Levy, Janey.
Refugee workers / Janey Levy.—1st ed.
p. cm.—(Extreme careers)
Includes bibliographical references and index.
ISBN-13: 978-1-4042-0960-2
ISBN-10: 1-4042-0960-3 (library binding)
1 Refugees—Services for—Juvenile literature. 2. Refugees—Juvenile literature. 3. Refugee camps—Juvenile literature. I. Title. II. Series.
HV640.L45 2007
362.87'53023—dc22

2006012519

Manufactured in the United States of America

On the cover: A medical worker talks to a refugee mother at Tug Wajale camp in the East African nation of Somalia. The camp was home to about 45,000 refugees who had fled persecution in neighboring Ethiopia.

Contents

Introduction 4

1 Uprooted and Suffering 8

2 Making a Difference 18

3 Refugee Work:
    Extreme Challenges 31

4 How to Become
    a Refugee Worker 44

Glossary 51

For More Information 54

For Further Reading 57

Bibliography 58

Index 62

Introduction

*T*he woman was at home when she heard the planes overhead. Her husband, two young sons, mother, and sister were there, too. The planes dropped bombs everywhere, and the family ran from the house in terror. The woman hasn't seen or heard from her husband since that day. She thinks he is probably dead or in prison. But her sons, mother, and sister escaped with her. Together, they set out to find someplace where they would be safe.

They walked for five days through hot, dry land with no food or water. One of her sons died of dehydration along the way. Finally they reached a camp. Here, they were safer. They had water, but there was not enough food. So the woman gathered wood and sold it in a nearby village. She used the *money to buy food for her family. And she waited and hoped for help.*

Who are this woman and her family? They are refugees. Refugees are people who have had to flee their homes and countries to escape conflict or persecution. When they flee, they leave behind friends—and perhaps family members. They are able to take with them only the few things they can carry. Refugees often wind up living in refugee camps with thousands of other people. For survival, they need basics such as food, water, shelter, and medical care. They also need protection from the dangers that forced them to flee. But they have no way to provide these things for themselves. Refugee workers therefore protect and provide aid until the refugees are able to build new lives.

Life as a refugee worker is difficult but rewarding. Refugee workers make a big difference in the lives of people who have been forced to leave everything behind. Some parts of the job are routine. Records have to be kept, so there is paperwork to do. But in most respects a refugee worker's job bears no resemblance to an office job. Often, the work is in faraway places and involves

In the 1990s, almost half a million people fled to Guinea, West Africa, to escape fighting in neighboring Sierra Leone and Liberia. The fighting spilled into Guinea in 2001, and many refugees were forced to flee again. These refugees at Katkama camp are waiting to be taken to a camp farther away from the fighting.

some risk. You might spend long periods of time in refugee camps. Camps may be in remote locations, and just getting there can be hazardous. Living conditions in camps are primitive, and the work is hard. There are also very real physical and psychological dangers. By being informed and prepared, you can take steps to reduce the dangers, but you can't eliminate them completely. To handle the different aspects of the job, you must be compassionate, resourceful, and able to work well with people from different national and cultural backgrounds. You also need to be strong, independent, and motivated to work under challenging conditions.

Uprooted and Suffering

1

You may have seen pictures of refugees on television or in a newspaper or magazine: long lines of desperate people fleeing on foot, or crowds huddled together in a refugee camp. They have been uprooted from their homes and forced to flee for their lives. Since they often must walk great distances, they can take with them only what they can easily carry. This may include some food, a few prized possessions, and any money they have. They leave behind homes, jobs, most of their belongings, friends, and perhaps family members. They don't know when or even if they will be able to return. It could be years, or it could be never. The danger that forced them to flee may never go away. Some may no longer have homes to return to. There are, unfortunately, millions of refugees today, all around the world.

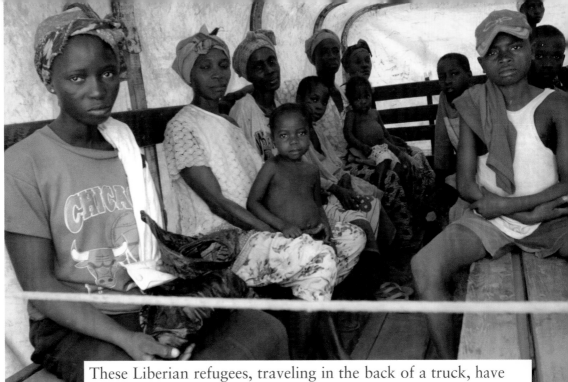

These Liberian refugees, traveling in the back of a truck, have just arrived at Largo camp in Sierra Leone. They have fled civil war in their home country. War first broke out in 1989 and lasted until 1996. New fighting began in 1999. Both sides in the war have been accused of terrible attacks against civilians.

Defining "Refugee"

You might be wondering exactly what qualifies a person as a refugee. International law defines refugees as people who have fled their home country and can't—or won't—return because they have good reason to fear being persecuted on the basis of their race, religion, nationality, political opinions, or membership in a

9

particular social group. People who are forced to flee because of natural disasters such as earthquakes and tsunamis are not considered refugees. Perhaps you've seen news stories about refugees escaping war or ethnic, tribal, or religious violence, however, and are surprised that this legal definition doesn't include them. Even though international law doesn't include people fleeing such conditions, the United Nations has said that these people should also be considered refugees, and they're usually treated as such.

Many different types of people become refugees. For instance, you might see entire families who are refugees. But as a rule, there are not many young or middle-aged men in groups of refugees. These men may be away fighting in a war, or may have been injured, killed, or taken prisoner. About 80 percent of refugees, therefore, are women, children, and elderly people. When you look at a group of refugees, you're likely to see lots of mothers with children. You'll also see women and elderly people alone. You might even see children alone.

In today's troubled world, refugees are found in more than 100 countries around the globe. Mercy Corps, a nonprofit organization that helps people in

About 200,000 Palestinian refugees in Lebanon live in camps like this one, which is just outside the city of Beirut. Plastic sheeting covers the rough huts. Poor sanitation and a lack of adequate and safe drinking water have caused serious health problems in the camps.

Refugee Camps Around the World

There are thousands of refugee camps. This list shows just a few of the major refugee camp locations and indicates where refugees in those camps come from.

Location of Refugee Camps	Home Country of Refugees
Thailand	Myanmar
Nepal	Bhutan
Iran	Afghanistan
Pakistan	Afghanistan
Tanzania	Burundi
Kenya	Somalia, Sudan
Chad	Sudan
Sierra Leone	Liberia
Ivory Coast	Liberia

need, estimates that there are currently around twelve million refugees. Others think there are as many as fourteen million. That's roughly equal to the number of people who live in the United States' two largest cities—New York City and Los Angeles. And that estimate doesn't include a related group of people known as "internally displaced persons."

Internally Displaced Persons

Internally displaced persons (IDPs) are like refugees, except that they remain in their home countries. IDPs, like refugees, have been forced to flee their homes because of persecution, war, or violence. But unlike refugees, IDPs haven't been displaced to another country. They've simply fled to another part of their homeland. Their movements have been internal, or inside their country.

There are currently approximately twenty-five million IDPs located throughout the world. That number is about double that of refugees—and roughly equal to the combined populations of the ten largest U.S. cities! Since IDPs haven't left their country, they're not officially refugees. Therefore, they traditionally haven't received the same kind of assistance that refugees have been given. The organizations that help refugees, however, are beginning to realize that IDPs need and deserve the same aid as refugees, and some organizations have begun to provide that aid. In fact, many people now even use the term "refugees" to refer to IDPs.

Life in a Refugee Camp

When refugees flee, they usually go to a neighboring country to seek asylum (safety). IDPs stay in their country but go as far away as possible from the dangers they faced at home. Sometimes, refugees and IDPs settle in cities or towns. Frequently, however, they wind up in large camps that have been set up especially for them. Refugee camps are often located in a neighboring country close to the border of the refugees' home country. Some camps are in remote locations that are difficult to reach.

Each camp houses thousands of people, who usually live crowded together. Camps range in size from about 10,000 to 500,000 people—the size of a small city! They are called camps because they have only tents or other simple shelters.

Living conditions in refugee camps range from difficult at best to downright primitive. Shelter may take the form of a piece of plastic sheeting or a simple hut made from

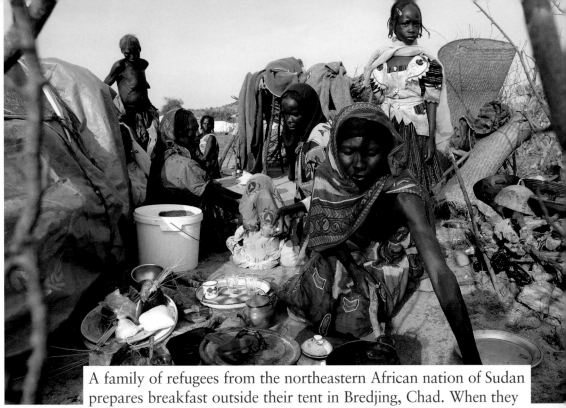

A family of refugees from the northeastern African nation of Sudan prepares breakfast outside their tent in Bredjing, Chad. When they arrived at the Bredjing camp, they joined about 12,000 other refugees living outside the camp. The camp, which was meant to hold 20,000 people, was already housing more than 37,000.

branches, leaves, or mud. Sometimes, refugees have no shelter at all. In some camps, refugees are fortunate enough to have tents to live in. But even then, life is far from comfortable. A large number of people may be crowded together in a single tent. Imagine thirteen people sharing a living space that's about ten feet wide and fifteen feet long—the size of an average bedroom. That's what it's like even in a good refugee camp.

Legal Definition of "Refugee"

The United Nations created the first legal definition of the term "refugee" in a 1951 document known as the Convention Relating to the Status of Refugees. A convention is an agreement between countries for regulating matters that affect all of them. The definition of "refugee" given on pages 9–10 comes from the 1951 Convention.

In some camps, refugees receive ready-made meals. But the food is not hot, and refugees may have to stand in line for hours to get it. In other camps, refugees get food that they have to cook for themselves. That way they can have a hot meal. But they may not have the utensils they need to cook the food. And they may have to leave the relative safety of the camp to look for firewood.

There may be a plentiful source of water in or near the camp, or people may have to stand in line for hours to get water. In some places, a family of ten people may receive only about one gallon of water per day.

All camps—from the best to the worst—are meant to be temporary homes. Unfortunately, it doesn't always work out that way. About seven million of the world's twelve to fourteen million refugees have been living in camps for more than ten years. However, the goal is to help refugees return to their homes as soon as it is safe to do so. This is called repatriation. Sometimes, however, repatriation isn't possible. The situation in their home country doesn't always improve, so refugees are not able to return, or they are afraid to. In that case, they may become permanent residents of the country they fled to. This is called local integration. Refugees may also seek to settle permanently in a third country, perhaps one farther away from their home. This is called resettlement. Regardless, throughout the refugees' whole experience—from their stays in camps through repatriation, local integration, or resettlement—they receive aid and protection from refugee workers.

Making a Difference

2

Pictures of refugees and stories of their suffering sometimes inspire people to take action. There are many ways to help. Some people donate money or supplies to an organization that aids refugees. Others want to take a more involved role, one that will put them right in the middle of the action, working directly with the refugees and facing the challenges of life in a refugee camp. They want to be refugee workers.

The Goal: To Protect Refugees

The primary goal of refugee workers is to protect refugees. This means making sure that refugees' human rights are respected and that they are not subject to new violence in the place where they've sought

These internally displaced Kurds carry as much as they can while fleeing fighting and persecution in Iraq. They are headed to safer locations high in the mountains of northern Iraq. American, British, and French soldiers helped to set up camps in the region for about half a million Kurds.

asylum. It also means making sure that they're not forced to return home when they still face danger there. Part of accomplishing these goals is making sure that refugees' basic needs are met. That may sound simple enough, but in reality it's a challenging job. Refugee camps are often in locations that are difficult to reach. It can be hard to get supplies to camps, and there may not be enough supplies to go around. Violence in and around camps may threaten

Angelina Jolie: Goodwill Ambassador

You may know Angelina Jolie as a famous movie star. But do you know about her work to help refugees? Jolie became interested in the plight of refugees while filming a movie in Cambodia. She went to the United Nations to find out what she could do to help. In 2001, the United Nations appointed Jolie as a UNHCR (United Nations High Commissioner for Refugees) Goodwill Ambassador.

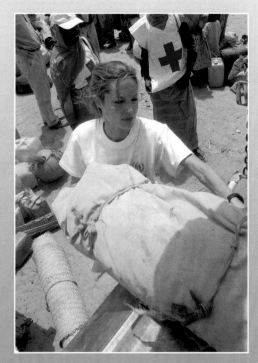

She has visited and helped at refugee camps in twenty countries, including Pakistan, Cambodia, Ecuador, Kosovo, Kenya, Tanzania, and Sudan. She has also met with government officials in many countries to promote refugee rights. In addition, she has participated in conferences around the world to talk about ways to help refugees.

On a visit to Chad, Angelina Jolie helps Sudanese refugees load their belongings onto a truck.

both refugee workers and refugees. These factors can make it a constant struggle for refugee workers to carry out their jobs.

What Refugee Workers Do

Refugee workers come from countries all over the world and have different types of backgrounds. There's a need for workers with a variety of skills because there are many tasks to be performed in refugee camps.

Some tasks are bureaucratic, or administrative. They are sometimes tedious but are necessary to organize a camp and make sure it runs as smoothly and fairly as possible. Record keeping and paperwork must be done. Systems for the distribution of food, shelter, and other basic supplies need to be established.

The Basics

One of the first tasks of refugee workers is to count refugees and register the size of each refugee family. This allows workers to determine what share of the resources each family gets. After registering the size of

Refugees from the central African nation of Rwanda crowd around two workers at Hongo camp in the Democratic Republic of the Congo. The workers, who are employed by an independent aid agency called CARE (Cooperative for Assistance and Relief Everywhere, Inc.), are counting and registering the refugees.

a refugee family, they give the family a ration card. The card notes how many people are in the family, which determines how much food the family receives. When refugees go to get food, they must present their ration card to the workers who distribute it.

If a natural water source does not exist near the camp, refugee workers may dig wells. If the region is so dry that wells can't produce sufficient water for the number of people in the camp, huge trucks may bring water to the camp. Refugee workers then distribute the water from the trucks. Workers also hand out items that provide shelter, such as tents or plastic sheeting, and perhaps blankets.

Hygiene and Health

If food, water, and shelter are the most basic needs for survival, hygiene and medical care are not far behind. Some refugee workers are specialists in sanitation and hygiene. They construct bathrooms and bathing areas, and try to keep the camp free of possible disease sources like dead animals.

Other workers are medical professionals, including doctors, who treat refugees

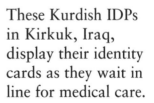

These Kurdish IDPs in Kirkuk, Iraq, display their identity cards as they wait in line for medical care.

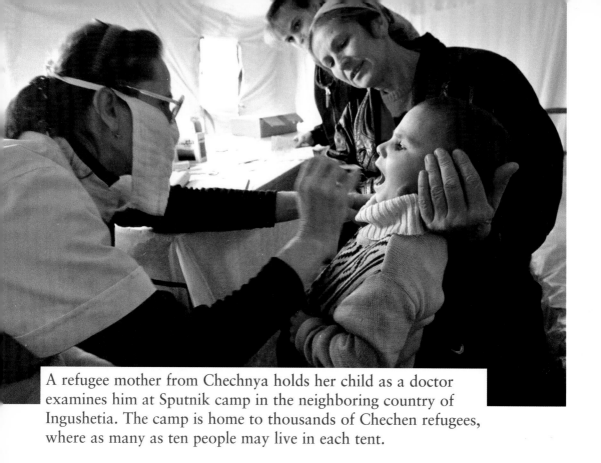

A refugee mother from Chechnya holds her child as a doctor examines him at Sputnik camp in the neighboring country of Ingushetia. The camp is home to thousands of Chechen refugees, where as many as ten people may live in each tent.

with health problems ranging from illness and injury to malnutrition and dehydration.

As you can imagine, refugees' physical health isn't the only thing that suffers due to the terrible circumstances they find themselves in. Their emotional and psychological health can also suffer. So, in addition to doctors and other medical professionals, there are counselors who help refugees cope with their experiences.

Education

Some workers teach children in the refugee camp. Others teach classes for women, who often had little or no education in their home countries. Some refugee workers even provide library services. You may think that library services sound like an "extra" that isn't particularly important, but workers believe that books specific to a refugee's background can offer significant benefits. The

books supply something familiar in an unfamiliar place and help refugees maintain their culture. This can improve refugees' spirits, which in turn can make it easier for them to begin the difficult task of rebuilding their lives.

In addition to general education, workers may also provide some specialized forms of education, including health care for women, and possibly even computer

A woman is teaching a class of Afghan girls at Shamshatu camp in Pakistan. The students sit on the floor because there is not enough money to buy desks or chairs.

classes. They may also provide training in skills such as weaving and candle making, for example, that refugees can use to earn income.

Helping Refugees with the Next Step

Since refugees are meant to stay in camps only temporarily, an important part of what workers do is help them with the next step. Most refugees hope for repatriation—they want to return home as soon as it is safe to do so. But if and when they do return, they will still need help. Their homes may have been destroyed and their jobs may be gone. Workers help refugees find solutions to these problems as they try to rebuild their lives.

When repatriation isn't possible, local integration is considered the next-best solution. Local integration requires working with the government of the host country. Refugee workers help to make these arrangements for the refugees to stay permanently.

Sometimes, though, neither repatriation nor local integration is a good option. In such cases, refugees hope to be able to resettle in a third country. This is the most difficult solution, and refugee workers have a variety of roles to play. Before refugees can be resettled, they must be approved by the government of that country. To get approval, they have to prove that their lives would be in danger if they returned to their home country. Refugee workers gather this evidence by conducting lengthy interviews with the refugees. They then prepare official paperwork to present the refugees' cases to the government.

Even after refugees have been accepted for resettlement, they still need help. Refugees are usually resettling

A long line of trucks carries Liberian refugees from camps in Sierra Leone back to Liberia. Repatriation was finally possible after war in Liberia ended in 2003. The sign on the lead truck wishes the refugees a safe journey home.

in countries where life is very different from what they're used to. To help them deal with these extreme changes, refugee workers teach special classes to prepare refugees for what life will be like in their new country.

Refugee Workers Outside of Camps

Refugee workers are stationed in other places besides refugee camps. They're found wherever there are refugees, including cities and rural settlements. There are many workers in the United States and other countries who aid refugees who have been resettled. Life in a new country can be overwhelming. These workers help refugees with the many practical and legal tasks they face as they build new lives. In the United States, for example, workers help refugees sign up for English classes and register their children in schools. They help refugees apply for Social Security cards, which the refugees will need to get jobs. They assist them in signing up for public programs like food stamps and medical insurance, which refugees will need to sustain them until they can find work. In addition, workers help refugees find jobs. They may even help refugees with routine activities such as grocery shopping. Refugee workers may also help to reunite families who were separated when they were forced to flee their homes.

Why Become a Refugee Worker?

Refugee workers have a hard, sometimes dangerous, job. And they don't get rich doing it. So why do people become refugee workers?

Some people become refugee workers because they've seen pictures of refugees and heard or read stories about their suffering, and want to help. Some people do it because they feel that they've been fortunate enough to enjoy a comfortable life, and they want to give something back to society. They want to help people who are suffering just because of where they happened to be born. Other refugee workers are people who were once refugees themselves. They know what it's like to flee their home in fear and try to build a new life somewhere else. They want to help those who are going through the same experience. Whatever the reason, all refugee workers want to make a difference in others' lives.

Refugee Work: Extreme Challenges

3

Imagine that it's 7:30 in the evening. You've just finished a simple dinner after working for ten hours. You still need to write a report and read over your notes from the day's meeting with refugees and workers from other agencies. Electricity will last only for about another hour. So you decide to work on your report while you have electricity. Then you'll read your notes by flashlight. You're covered with dust after a long, hot day, and you'd like to take a shower. But you can't because the water system isn't working. Instead, you'll go straight to bed, making sure that the mosquito net around your bed is in place. Mosquitoes carry diseases, and you don't want to get bitten. You hear gunfire in the distance. It will probably continue for hours. It's just another day in your life as a refugee worker.

Living Conditions

Refugee workers don't actually live in the camps. Instead, they live nearby. Living conditions for workers vary from camp to camp, depending on the resources available. The conditions are usually better than they are for refugees, but are still very modest. In some camps, for example, workers may live together in a rough brick structure with a straw roof. There might be a few basic pieces of furniture. Mosquito nets or plastic sheeting may serve as curtains. Electricity is probably provided by a generator, but it's likely not available twenty-four hours a day. There may be a water pump that supplies water from a nearby well. The water supply is likely to be limited, though, which means that bathing and clothes washing are probably infrequent. Meals are usually simple, and may be prepared with local fruits and vegetables. Computers may be needed to keep records, write reports, and analyze disease data. Other equipment will likely be necessary to perform jobs such as providing health care. It can be difficult, however, to get the computers and equipment. Days likely begin early and end late.

Yvan Sturm, a UNHCR worker, has spent a long day visiting Sudanese refugees at camps in Chad. Still, his work is not done. By lamplight, he uses his satellite phone to download e-mails to his laptop computer.

All in a Day's Work

When a camp is being set up, one of the first tasks is to count refugees, register families, and issue ration cards. Refugees wait their turn, usually in a large tent. The sheer numbers can make this job seem overwhelming. More than 7,000 refugees might come through a tent in a single day! Workers count the number of people in a family and issue a ration card for that many people.

Workers may also decide what constitutes a family. Perhaps a mother and father want to divorce and split up their seven children. Workers have to decide whether this is one family of nine people or two separate families, one with five people and one with four people. Or an elderly person might come in with four children. Perhaps one child is the elderly person's grandchild and the other three are orphans who have no one else to care for them. Workers may decide they are a family and give them one ration card for a family of five.

The refugees are all desperate, and some may ask for additional ration cards or try to cheat by going through the line twice and getting extra cards that way. It can be hard to say no to people who have lost so much. Workers must keep in mind what resources are available and what is most fair for everyone.

The number of people in a family may change later as more refugees arrive. So workers might have to go to every tent or shelter in the camp to recount the number of people in each family and make sure the family has a ration card for the right number of people. This can take a long time. Suppose the camp has 100,000 refugees and each tent or shelter has an average of ten people in it. That's 10,000 tents or shelters that need to be visited!

Medical Care

The number of medical professionals at a refugee camp varies. Some camps might have several, while other camps might only have one or none at all. Medical professionals spend their days at the camp clinic seeing patients—sometimes up to 100 a day. Some refugees have minor illnesses or injuries that are easy to treat, but many have more serious health problems. Equipment and medicines are not always available, so it can be difficult to treat patients. When people are too sick to come to the clinic, a medical professional

Touloum Refugee Camp

About 16,000 refugees from Sudan live in Touloum camp in eastern Chad. There is a school tent, complete with blackboards, where refugee workers teach the camp's children. Among the subjects taught is English. The camp also has a medical center and residential areas. Refugee workers designed the residential space to mimic the refugees' home villages. Groups of eight tents are arranged in circles around common areas.

will go to see them. The sickest people may or may not be sent to a hospital somewhere else. Some of the patients will die. If the camp is short on food, water, and medicine, as many as fifty people may die each day.

Food

The United Nations World Food Programme and other humanitarian organizations donate food and deliver it to refugee camps. Refugee workers distribute the food, but not on a daily basis. Sometimes, food is distributed every two weeks. Sometimes, it's distributed as infrequently as once a month. Workers also monitor the food supplies and make sure they have everything they need. They communicate with the organizations that provide the food. When food is delivered, they make sure it's stored properly in the camp warehouse.

Camp Hygiene

Some workers help maintain sanitation and hygiene in the camp. They perform routine tasks such as setting up communal baths and bathrooms for the refugees. They also perform less-routine tasks. For example, refugees in

A United Nations worker throws bags of flour to the Palestinian refugees gathering around the food distribution truck at Dheisheh camp in the Israeli-occupied West Bank.

some areas may bring donkeys with them because they're valuable work animals. They may bring other animals as well, such as goats and dogs. If there is not enough water in the camp for both people and animals, many animals will die. The dead animals' bodies must be collected and burned so they don't become a health hazard. Workers may spend up to six days a week collecting and burning animals' bodies.

Resettlement

Some workers help refugees who are seeking resettlement. Refugees who want to resettle need to be interviewed. After these interviews, workers determine whether the people qualify for resettlement. If so, paperwork is prepared that presents their case. Long lines of refugees wait to see resettlement workers every day. Each case takes at least eight hours to prepare, so, unfortunately, there is simply not enough time to help everyone.

Once refugees have been chosen for resettlement, they will need to help prepare for life in the country to which they will relocate. They will need help learning the language spoken in their new country, as well as

Hmong refugees at Wat Tham Krabok camp in Thailand attend a cultural orientation class. They are part of a large group of Hmong refugees from Laos who will be resettled in the United States. The class is designed to teach them about life in the United States, which will be very different from life in Laos and Thailand.

many other things. The life they're used to may be completely different from what it will be like in the United States or another Western country. They need to learn about the culture of their new country. If a refugee is going to move to the United States, for example, he or she may attend classes about life in the United States. Refugee workers might also teach them about U.S. laws, work, and transportation, as well as about money, making a budget, and paying bills.

Meetings

In order to make a camp the best it can be, and provide the greatest aid possible to refugees, everyone in the camp needs to figure out how to work together. Workers need to know the refugees' needs and concerns. So workers spend time meeting with the refugees' leaders, who are usually men. Workers also spend time with women and girls in the camp to learn about their specific needs and concerns.

In each camp, there are usually several different agencies involved in helping refugees. Refugee workers from these agencies meet to discuss what each agency is doing, possible problems they're having, and how the agencies can best work together to help the refugees.

Risks

Daily life for refugee workers includes many risks. Some are physical, and disease is always a danger. The risk of disease can be reduced, however, by getting any necessary vaccinations before going to a remote place, and by taking medications that help prevent certain diseases. Workers who spend time with people who have contagious diseases should wear protective gear. It is also important for workers to take care of themselves by eating right and getting enough sleep.

Violence is another danger. Violence may occur inside the camp. While most refugees are innocent victims, some are not. Occasionally, former soldiers or criminals might attack workers. Violence may also come from outside the camp. If fighting is taking place nearby, the camp could be attacked. This

Unrest in the Bredjing Refugee Camp

Bredjing camp in Chad was meant to house 20,000 refugees from Sudan, but in 2004 it contained twice that many. That meant the camp was much more crowded than even a "normal" refugee camp. The crowding raised stress levels for refugees and workers alike, and caused extra problems such as finding enough water for everyone. As a result of these factors, unrest broke out in the camp, and the military of Chad had to come in to control it. Two people were killed. Once calm was restored, new security measures were set up in the camp to prevent similar problems from occurring again.

Many factors can trigger violence that can make a camp unsafe. For example, refugees' resentment about their situation may erupt into violence. Here, young Palestinians throw stones at an Israeli armored vehicle in the West Bank refugee camp of Ein Beit Ilma.

actually happened to refugee camps in the Democratic Republic of the Congo in 1996. Fighters outside the camp may try to get refugees in the camp to join the fighting, and they may even give weapons to the refugees. This has also happened at camps in Côte d'Ivoire (the Ivory Coast).

Refugee workers can reduce the dangers from violence by exercising common sense. Inside and outside the camp, it is important to stay with other workers. They also keep walkie-talkies charged and handy so they are able to reach other workers if they need help. If the dangers become too great, agencies may remove all their workers from a camp.

There are also psychological risks. Refugee workers may experience frustration at being unable to help everyone or being unable to deliver aid as quickly as it's needed. This can lead to depression and, ultimately, to burnout. Experts are encouraging agencies to do more to help workers deal with these risks by providing better training and support.

How to Become a Refugee Worker

4

Refugee workers' jobs are with one of the various humanitarian agencies that aid refugees. But just what are these agencies?

The UNHCR is one of the world's principal humanitarian agencies. Since it was created in 1950, the agency has helped more than fifty million people. Its primary purpose is to guard the welfare of refugees and protect their rights. It also works with governments and other agencies and institutions around the world to try to prevent the situations that create refugees. About 6,500 people work for the UNHCR worldwide, providing assistance to refugees and IDPs in more than 100 countries.

Independent international aid agencies also employ refugee workers. Because these agencies are not part of

A family of Afghan refugees receives money from a UNHCR worker after returning to Afghanistan from Pakistan. The UNHCR is one of the world's largest agencies devoted to helping refugees and IDPs.

a government and were not founded by a government, they're called nongovernmental organizations, or NGOs. They're also sometimes called private voluntary organizations, or PVOs. The Red Cross and CARE (Cooperative for Assistance and Relief Everywhere, Inc.) are two well-known NGOs. While not all NGOs provide aid to refugees and IDPs—some are devoted to causes like the environment, economic development, and human rights—many do. Since women and children

The International Rescue Committee

Even before the UNHCR was founded in 1950, there were NGOs working to help refugees. One such NGO is the International Rescue Committee (IRC), which was founded in 1933. Its initial mission was to help Germans who were being persecuted by Germany's Nazi government. Today, the IRC is one of the world's leading NGOs and provides aid to refugees and IDPs in about twenty-five countries.

usually suffer the most in the situations that create refugees and IDPs, some organizations even focus specifically on providing them with aid.

Churches and religious organizations may also employ refugee workers. These groups often focus their efforts on assisting refugees who have been resettled. Workers employed by them are therefore less likely to work abroad in camps.

Becoming a Refugee Worker: Education

Refugee workers need a good education. They must be able to communicate well, both verbally and in writing. They also need to speak at least one other language besides English. Basic math skills, at the very least, are important, as are analytical skills. Knowledge of geography and an understanding of different cultures and ways of life are crucial. Since challenging situations and problems often present themselves to refugee workers, it is necessary to have the ability to find creative solutions.

Refugee workers must have a college education. There is no one field of study that is best for a career as a refugee worker. There are several, however, that are generally regarded as providing good background. These fields include international studies, religious studies, and anthropology (the study of the origin and behavior of humans and the development of societies and cultures). Post-college study can include a graduate degree in humanitarian assistance. But it is not necessary to pursue one of these fields of study. Refugee workers perform many different jobs, and some require very specialized skills. Expertise in engineering, medicine, and law, for example, are all needed in refugee work.

Practical Experience

Practical experience is helpful for refugee workers. Many humanitarian agencies have opportunities for volunteers,

Volunteer Work

It is possible to get a taste of life as a refugee worker by volunteering. Workers in refugee camps are usually paid professionals. But NGOs, churches, and religious organizations sometimes use volunteers to help with refugees who have been resettled. These volunteers receive special training before they start work. Check with these agencies to see if there are any volunteer opportunities in your community.

and some accept interns. An intern is a student who gains valuable practical experience while working under the supervision of a professional. Interns might conduct research, prepare reports, organize meetings, or write material about refugees for the agency's Web site. This kind of experience is helpful for finding a job, as well as for being better prepared to carry out its duties.

Another way to get experience is to join the Peace Corps after college or graduate school. The Peace Corps is an agency of the federal government that was established in 1961 to promote world peace and friendship. Peace Corps volunteers work in more than 135 countries around the world, providing help with education, health, community development, agriculture, environment, and information technology. Peace Corps volunteers

Joshua Fuder *(right)* joined the Peace Corps after graduating from college with a degree in international studies. He volunteers in Vanuatu, a group of islands in the Pacific Ocean near Australia. Here, Fuder talks to a local man who was forced to leave his home because of fears that a nearby volcano would erupt.

don't provide aid to refugees and IDPs, but their experiences are in many ways similar to those of refugee workers. They live in a foreign country where life is very different from what they're used to. They work with people from different backgrounds, often in challenging circumstances. And their work requires many of the same skills and qualities that refugee workers must have.

Now You're Ready

After college and some practical work experience, people can apply to become refugee workers. When an agency hires someone, it provides training before sending the new employee out in the field as a refugee worker.

Refugee work is not the right career for everyone. But for someone who wants to make a difference in the lives of uprooted people and wants to do challenging work under difficult conditions, it can be a satisfying and rewarding choice.

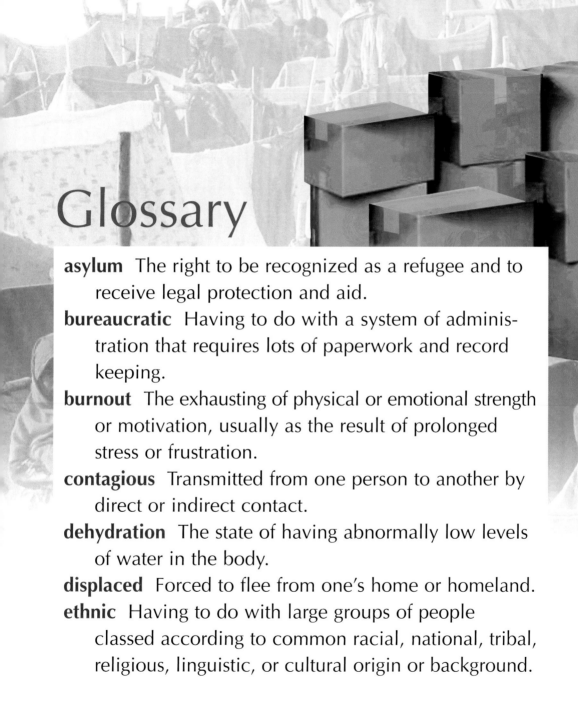

Glossary

asylum The right to be recognized as a refugee and to receive legal protection and aid.

bureaucratic Having to do with a system of administration that requires lots of paperwork and record keeping.

burnout The exhausting of physical or emotional strength or motivation, usually as the result of prolonged stress or frustration.

contagious Transmitted from one person to another by direct or indirect contact.

dehydration The state of having abnormally low levels of water in the body.

displaced Forced to flee from one's home or homeland.

ethnic Having to do with large groups of people classed according to common racial, national, tribal, religious, linguistic, or cultural origin or background.

generator A machine that is usually portable and produces electricity.

humanitarian Promoting human welfare and social reform.

human rights Rights that are considered by most societies to belong to all people, such as rights to freedom, justice, and equality.

hygiene Conditions or practices that promote health.

integration The act or process of incorporating a group of people into a society as equals.

malnutrition Lack of adequate nutrition to maintain health.

mosquito net A net or screen used to keep out mosquitoes.

persecution The act or practice of punishing people or treating them badly because they belong to a different race or ethnic group, or have a different religion or political or social ideas.

psychological Having to do with the functioning of the mind.

ration A share of food as determined by the supply or total available amount.

repatriation The act or process of returning a refugee to his or her home country.

resettlement The act or process of helping a refugee move to a distant country and establish a new life.

sanitation The promotion of hygiene and disease prevention by removing garbage and human waste.

uproot To displace from a country or traditional home area.

vaccination An injection of organisms that produces or increases resistance to a particular disease.

For More Information

Canadian Council for Refugees
6839 rue Drolet #302
Montreal, QC H2S 2T1
Canada
(514) 277-7223
Web site: http://www.web.net/~ccr

InterAction
1717 Massachusetts Avenue NW, Suite 701
Washington, D.C. 20036
(202) 667-8227
Web site: http://www.interaction.org

International Committee of the Red Cross (ICRC)
19 Avenue de la Paix
CH 1202 Geneva

Switzerland
Web site: http://www.icrc.org

International Rescue Committee (IRC)
122 East 42nd Street
New York, NY 10168-1289
(212) 551-3000
Web site: http://www.theirc.org

Peace Corps
Paul D. Coverdell Peace Corps Headquarters
1111 20th Street NW
Washington, D.C. 20526
(800) 424-8580
Web site: http://www.peacecorps.gov

United Nations High Commissioner for Refugees (UNHCR)
Case Postale 2500
CH-1211 Genève 2 Dépôt
Switzerland
Web site: http://www.unhcr.org

USA for UNHCR
1775 K Street NW, Suite 290
Washington, D.C. 20006
(800) 770-1100 or (202) 296-1115
Web site: http://www.usaforunhcr.org

**Women's Commission for Refugee Women
and Children**
122 East 42nd Street
New York, NY 10168-1289
(212) 551-3000
Web site: http://www.womenscommission.org

Web Sites

Due to the changing nature of Internet links, Rosen Publishing has developed an online list of Web sites related to the subject of this book. This site is updated regularly. Please use this link to access the list:

http://www.rosenlinks.com/ec/rewo

For Further Reading

Burger, Leslie, and Debra L. Rahm. *United Nations High Commissioner for Refugees: Making a Difference in Our World.* Minneapolis, MN: Lerner Publishing Group, 1996.

Jolie, Angelina. *Notes from My Travels: Visits with Refugees in Africa, Cambodia, Pakistan, and Ecuador.* New York, NY: Pocket Books, 2003.

Naidoo, Beverly. *Making It Home: Real-Life Stories from Children Forced to Flee.* New York, NY: Puffin Books, 2005.

Parry, Ann. *Doctors Without Borders* (Humanitarian Organizations). New York, NY: Chelsea House Publishers, 2005.

Williams, Mary. *Brothers in Hope: The Story of the Lost Boys of Sudan.* New York, NY: Lee & Low Books, 2005.

Bibliography

Clark, Jennifer. "Diaries from the Field." USA for UNHCR.
    Retrieved December 9, 2005 (http://www.usaforunhcr.
    org/dynamic.cfm?ID=230).

French, Howard W. "Zaire Government Is Arming
    Hutus, Making Human Shields of Refugees." *New
    York Times*, February 19, 1997. Retrieved
    December 1, 2005 (http://www.hartford-hwp.com/
    archives/35/100.html).

Human Rights Watch. "Youth, Blood and Poverty: The
    Lethal Legacy of West Africa's Regional Warriors: IV.
    The Recruiters, Their Promises, the Lure." Retrieved
    December 18, 2005 (http://hrw.org/reports/2005/
    westafrica0405/4.htm).

International Rescue Committee. "History of the Inter-
    national Rescue Committee." Retrieved December 27,
    2005 (http://www.theirc.org/about/history.html).

IRIN. UN Office for the Coordination of Humanitarian Affairs. "Sierra Leone: Liberian Child Soldiers Still Make Trouble Without Guns." Retrieved December 1, 2005 (http://www.irinnews.org/webspecials/childsoldiers/SierraLeone031203.asp).

Jolie, Angelina. "Sudan Journal." United Nations High Commissioner for Refugees. Retrieved November 21, 2005 (http://www.unhcr.org/cgi-bin/texis/vtx/help/opendoc.htm?tbl=HELP&id=439d4ee52).

Miller, T. Christian, and Ann M. Simmons. "Relief Camps for Africans and Kosovars: Worlds Apart." *Los Angeles Times*, May 21, 1999. Retrieved November 19, 2005 (http://www.transnational.org/features/contrasts.html).

Online NewsHour. "Refugee Crisis in Sudan." Retrieved November 30, 2005 (http://www.pbs.org/newshour/bb/africa/jan-june04/refugees_05-13.html).

P.O.V. "Lost Boys of Sudan: In Search of the 'Durable Solution': The Refugee Situation Today." Retrieved December 1, 2005 (http://www.pbs.org/pov/pov2004/lostboysofsudan/special_interviews.html).

Salama, Peter. "The Psychological Health of Relief Workers: Some Practical Suggestions."

Humanitarian Practice Network. Retrieved November 18, 2005 (http://www.odihpn.org/report. asp?ID=1043).

Solomon, Alisa. "The Golden Ticket: Will Our Refugee Program Survive 9-11 and the Breakup of the INS?" *Village Voice*, May 8–14, 2002. Retrieved November 18, 2005 (http://www.villagevoice.com/ news/0219,solomon,34588,1.html).

Takafumi, Miyake. "Libraries for Refugee Camps: The Shanti Volunteer Association." Retrieved December 18, 2005 (http://www.accu.or.jp/appreb/09/pdf33-1/ 33-1p009-011.pdf).

United Nations High Commissioner for Refugees. "Basic Facts." Retrieved November and December 2005 (http://www.unhcr.org/cgi-bin/texis/vtx/basics).

United Nations High Commissioner for Refugees. "How You Can Help: Angelina Jolie, UNHCR Goodwill Ambassador." Retrieved November 19, 2005 (http:// www.unhcr.org/cgi-bin/texis/vtx/help?id=3f94ff664).

United Nations Population Fund. "Local Women's NGOs Play Crucial Role for Afghan Refugee Women." Retrieved November 30, 2005 (http://www.unfpa.org/ news/news.cfm?ID=202&Language=1).

USA for UNHCR. "Action: What You Can Do to Help." Retrieved December 9, 2005 (http://www. usaforunhcr.org/a_action.cfm).

Whitaker, Beth Elise. "First Person: Faces in the Crowd: Counting Heads and Deciding Fates in a Camp for Rwandan Refugees." *Princeton Alumni Weekly*, October 23, 1996. Retrieved November 19, 2005 (http://www.princeton.edu/~paw/archive_old/ PAW96-97/03-1023/1023endpg.html).

Women's Commission for Refugee Women and Children. "Profiles of Courage." Retrieved December 1, 2005 (http://www.womenscommission.org/projects/P&P/ af/awf_profile.shtml).

Zwerdling, Daniel. "Blood and Oil in Burma." American RadioWorks. Retrieved November 30, 2005 (http://americanradioworks.publicradio.org/ features/burma/).

Index

A
asylum, 14, 19

B
Bredjing refugee camp, 41

C
CARE, 45

D
Democratic Republic of the
    Congo, 42
disease, 23, 31, 32, 40, 41

G
Goodwill Ambassador,
    UNHCR, 20

H
human rights, 18, 44, 45
hygiene, 23, 36

I
integration, 17, 27
internally displaced persons
    (IDPs), 13, 14, 25, 44, 45,
    46, 49
International Rescue Committee
    (IRC), 46

J
Jolie, Angelina, 20

M
Mercy Corps, 10

N
nongovernmental organizations
    (NGOs), 45–46, 48

O
Office of the United Nations High
    Commissioner for Refugees
    (UNHCR), 20, 25, 44, 46

P

Peace Corps, 48–49
persecution, 5, 9, 13
private voluntary organizations
    (PVOs), 45

R

ration cards, 22, 33–34
Red Cross, 45
refugee camps
    education in, 25–26, 35
    food/water in, 16, 22–23,
        34, 36
    hygiene/sanitation in, 23,
        36–38
    living conditions in, 7,
        14–15, 32
    long-term stays in, 16–17
    major locations of, 12
    medical care in, 23–24,
        35–36
    violence in, 19–21, 41–43
refugees
    basic needs of, 5, 14, 16, 19,
        22, 23, 29, 35-36, 40, 41
    crowded conditions at camps,
        8, 14, 15, 33, 41
    dangers facing, 5, 8, 13, 14,
        19, 41–42
    definition of, 5, 9–10, 16
    education of, 25–26, 28, 29,
        35, 38–39
    number of, 5, 8, 12, 13, 16,
        33, 35
    types of, 10, 34, 45–46
refugee worker
    administrative duties, 5, 21–22,
        27, 29, 31, 33–34, 38, 40
    definition of, 5, 18
    emotional toll on, 7, 43
    ensuring refugee safety, 5, 17, 18
    living conditions, 7, 31, 32,
        41, 46
    motivation for becoming a,
        18, 30
    providing health care, 23–24,
        25, 32, 35–36
    qualifications for, 7, 21,
        46–47, 49
    supplying basic needs, 5, 17,
        19, 21, 22–23, 36, 41
    training of, 43, 48, 50
    work risks of, 7, 19, 29, 31,
        40–43, 49
repatriation, 17, 26, 27
resettlement, 17, 27, 29, 38–39,
    46, 48

S

sanitation, 23, 36
Sudan, 20, 41

T

Touloum refugee camp, 35

U

United Nations, 10, 16, 20, 25
   World Food Programme, 36

V

violence, 10, 13, 18, 19, 41–42
volunteers/interns, 47–48

W

water, obtaining, 16, 22–23,
   32, 36

About the Author

Janey Levy is an editor and author, and has written more than fifty books for young people. She regularly supports the work of the International Rescue Committee and Doctors Without Borders, two NGOs that provide critical aid to refugees around the world. She lives in Colden, New York.

Photo Credits

Cover © Peter Turnley/Corbis; p. 6 © Christine Nesbit/AP/Wide World Photos; p. 9 © Natalie Behring-Chisholm/Getty Images; p. 11 © Marco Di Lauro/ Getty Images; p. 15 © Scott Nelson/Getty Images; p.19 Patrick Baz/AFP/Getty Images; p.20 © Edward Parsons/AFP/Getty Images; p. 22 © Howard Davies/ Corbis; p. 23 © Getty Images; p. 24 © Musa Sadulayev/AP/Wide World Photos; p. 26 © Chris Hondros/Getty Images; p. 28 © Pewee Flomoku/AP/ Wide World Photos; p. 33 © UNHCR/H. Caux; p. 37 © Tim Russo/Getty Images; p. 39 © Paula Bronstein/Getty Images; p. 42 © Jaafar Ashtiyeh/ AFP/ Getty Images; p. 45 © Shah Marai/AFP/Getty Images; p.49 © Rick Rycroft/AP/ Wide World Photos.

Editor: Liz Gavril; Photo Research: Hillary Arnold